# KIDS RULE THE WORLD

### SUSAN TODD

**PRESENTED TO:**

_____

**FROM:**

_____

**DATE:**

_____

## NOTES:

**Production Team**

*Cover & Interior Design
& Photography:*
VIP Graphics
St. Louis, MO

*Cover Concept:*
Jen Marmarinos
David Vordtriede

*Cover Models:*
Kim Corpuz
Robert Johnson
Emily McGillem

*Proofreading:*
Gina Keckritz
GinaKeckritz@cs.com

**Publisher:**
EFG, Inc.
St. Louis, MO
quicknews@aol.com

*Distributed to the
trade by:*
**Writer's Digest Books**
An Imprint of F&W Publications
1507 Dana Ave.,
Cincinnati, OH 45207
(800) 289-0963;
(513) 531-2690
fax (513) 531-4082

## DEDICATION

To the over 6,000 kids worldwide who have contributed to the kidnews.com site since 1995. Also, to Dr. Peter Owens who had the vision for kidnews.com and to Tara Davis who keeps the site alive and vibrant.

## ACKNOWLEDGEMENTS

Thanks to the newspaper journalists at New Directions for News and the librarians, booksellers and publishers at BookExpo whose eyes lit up when they saw this project.

Thanks to the F&W Publications team who've provided feedback over the last two years on this project— Stacie Berger, Christine Carli, Sally Finnegan, Jack Heffron, Steve Koenig, Liz Koffel, David Lewis, Mary Poggione, Laura Smith, David Swan, Joanne Widmer and the F&W field sales team. Special thanks to Richard Hunt for naming this book.

**Kids Rule the World**: An Interactive Internet Writing Kit.

Library of Congress Catalog Card Number 01-107521

ISBN: 1-930500-30-0

First Edition: Printed and bound in the USA.

04    03    02    01    00    5    4    3    2    1

# TABLE OF CONTENTS

## KIDS WHO RULE

Each chapter of the book includes boxes marked, "Kids Who Rule." These are stories of other kids and how they've used writing and community involvement to make the world a better place.

3

# WELCOME TO KIDS RULE THE WORLD!

This book came to be because of kids, parents and teachers who actively used the kidnews.com Web site. The site was started in February 1995 by Dr. Peter Owens, professor of journalism at the University of Massachusetts, Dartmouth.

Dr. Owens believes that when kids write like journalists do —interview people, write about their opinions and write reviews— they become more active citizens and build powerful local, regional and worldwide communities. In short, by using their editorial voices, kids rule!

This is what the kidnews.com site looks like:

## KIDS WHO RULE

In a poll of 2,000 kids from almost 90 countries, kids ages 8 to 15 were asked to define the biggest challenge they faced in making a difference in their communities. The number one response was: "Not taken seriously by adults."

The poll was part of the Millennium Dreamers Symposium, presented by McDonald's Corp. Disney and UNESCO.

4

## HOW TO USE THIS BOOK & CD

This book is filled with writing activities that you *do*, *write* and then *publish* in kidnews.com or other places. The chapters of the book follow the sections on the kidnews.com site. Each chapter has its own icon for the activity type—Advice & Opinions, Reviews, Creative, Features, Sports and News. You'll see the same icons and sections when you go online to the kidnews.com site.

When a worksheet appears in the book, you'll also see a box in the sidebar with the title "Using the CD." The box lists where to find the form on the CD. Use these forms to help you think of ideas, take notes, organize your thoughts and polish your writing.

## USING THE KIDNEWS.COM SITE

When you select an activity to do, follow the instructions written in the book. Once you've collected your information and thoughts and are ready to write, get online and go to the kidnews.com site for examples of writing from other kids. Here you'll see which styles and subjects you like. Note what makes you want to read a story—the headlines, the first sentence, the length, etc.

## SUBMITTING WRITING TO KIDNEWS.COM

Send your stories to kidnews.com by going to www.kidnews.com and clicking on the "Submit writing" button. If you've already written your story on the computer, copy the text and paste it into the "Enter your text" area. Please make sure that the "caps lock" button is off on your computer. Your submission will be returned if it's typed in all capital letters. Include your other information on the form. Please note that your e-mail address is completely private when submitted to kidnews.com.

Each submission is looked at by our editor. (Don't worry—she's really nice.) Then, wait about a week and check back to the site to see your name in print!

### USING THE CD

The forms on the CD are in pdf format that can be opened and printed using Adobe Acrobat Reader. If you don't have the reader on your computer, download it at www.adobe.com

### NOTES:

Even though the CD included with this book is the size and shape of a credit card, it can be safely read by the CD-ROM drive on your computer.

5

## SURFING SAFELY

Throughout the book you'll see a yellow computer in the margin that tells about a site to go to or gives you tips for searching online. Before you go online, read the following tips provided by the editor of kidnews.com, Tara Davis.

*Safety Tip #1*: Never give out personal information about yourself. That includes your last name, your phone number or your home address. Do not post it on bulletin boards or newsgroups, and do not fill out any application forms without your parents' or guardian's permission. It is perfectly acceptable to use an alias or nickname.

*Kids Safety Tip #2*: Be suspicious of anyone who asks you for personal information. If someone makes you uncomfortable, tell your parents, stop all contact with that person and delete any mail you get from them. Do not be afraid to tell your parents or guardian.

*Kids Safety Tip #3*: Ask your parents or guardian before posting your e-mail address. They can surf with you and check to make sure the place you are posting is appropriate.

*Kids Safety Tip #4*: People are not always what they seem online. There are a lot of good people out there, right along with the bad ones. Meeting people from the Internet is not a good idea at all; don't even give them your phone number or address. However, if you decide you want to anyway, ask your parents or guardian to make plans with you and go with you to a public place. NEVER do any of this alone.

*Kids Safety Tip #5*: Don't open up any e-mail or attached files or Web pages that you receive from people you don't know. If it looks suspicious or odd, delete it or ask an adult to look at it first.

*Kids Safety Tip #6*: Passwords are secret so don't give yours out to anyone except an adult you trust in your home.

*Kids Safety Tip #7*: If a Web page looks suspicious or has a warning about you being underage, leave immediately. Avoid chatrooms that look suspicious or are not geared towards kids.

## ADDITIONAL SAFETY TIPS

In addition to the tips listed, here are a few more ideas for parents, teachers and guardians.

*Tip #1*: There is no substitute for you! Sit down with your kids and surf the Internet together. While you spend time letting them teach you about the computer, you can teach them how to be responsible and safe. They may know more about bits and bytes, but you are still the guide for the social aspect of the online world.

*Tip #2*: Show your kids how to surf safely. There are numerous software tools that filter out things you don't want your children exposed to and they are quite effective.

*Tip #3*: Make sure the kids know it is okay to come get you if they receive a strange e-mail that makes them uncomfortable or they accidentally get to a site you have told them is not appropriate. Let them know that you won't get angry and that it isn't their fault if they do get something strange or they find a site by accident. Establish the ground rules and let the kids know clearly what they are. Every family is different and every child is an individual, so there are no 'magic rules' to follow beyond the basics. The more open you are and the more you listen, the more likely they are to tell you what is going on.

*Tip #4*: Eventually, you or your child might want to meet someone you have been corresponding with for sometime. It will come up sooner or later; but if the kids are not afraid to ask questions they probably won't be sneaking around to do it without you. Meeting someone from online is a personal decision and should be approached with caution. Never meet the people alone and always meet in a public place. You might even want to start with a phone call. If two children want to meet, each child should have an adult supervisor. You can arrange with the other child's supervisor to talk and make the arrangements to get together.

### GO SURFING

If you're working on a classroom, school or writing club collection, check out some other writing collections and newspapers at:
www.kidnews.com/goodies.html

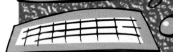

7

# ADVICE & OPINIONS

BLAH BLAH BLAH

## CHAPTER MAP

In this chapter you'll learn how to write opinions and editorials. Writing ideas include:

- Explaining what's wrong with school
- Telling adults what they need to know
- Looking into what kids worry about

## NOTES:

**Opinions**

Your opinion is something that you believe but no one can prove and that may not be true for everyone.

Kids know and care a lot about issues and events in the world. When you write advice and opinions, you get a chance to talk about the ideas and problems that make you happy, sad, mad, glad, worried, hopeful, afraid, proud, scared or excited.

Opinions are ideas and feelings about facts. If everybody at your school has to take three years of math classes, that's a fact. If you think math is easy and fun, that's your opinion.

When news writers want to put in their opinions about hard news, they write *editorials*. An editorial shows the writer's opinion about a news subject and is written to persuade readers to do something or to feel a certain way.

Here are some examples of opinion stories or editorials:

⭐ Smoking is dangerous, so kids should never try it.

⭐ People should recycle their trash.

⭐ Students should be in school all year long, so they don't forget what they've learned over the summer.

These can be argued because they have at least two sides. Even if most people would agree with the opinion in the story (like in the one about smoking), it's still an opinion.

If you give *advice*, you're using your opinion to help people solve problems. If a friend is having trouble getting along with somebody at school, you might offer some suggestions to fix the problem. You're offering advice.

We've put advice and opinions together because in both of them you give your opinion and back it up with facts and suggestions.

## HOW TO WRITE ADVICE AND OPINIONS

- Pick something that you care about. When you choose a topic and already care about it, your writing will be interesting to you and your reader.

- Learn more about it. Do some research in books or on the Web to make your discussion stronger.

- Find out what other people think, even if they disagree with you. It's easier to argue something if you understand the other side.

- Include plenty of emotions to show your readers that you care about what you're discussing.

- Back up your opinions with facts to show why you feel the way you do.

- If you're giving advice, it can be helpful if you've been through the situation.

- Remember to respect other people's opinions.

- Read the writing of other kids by going to the Advice & Opinions section at www.kidnews.com.

In addition to the following activities, also consider:

**Sibling Stress**: Think about problems you have had with a brother or a sister and what you have learned from those problems. Use the causes and solutions to help other kids get along better with their siblings.

**Report Card Recommendations**: Give advice to other kids about making better grades, or offer suggestions to teachers or parents about helping kids do better in school.

**Words of Wisdom**: Help other kids by offering advice for things like how to handle peer pressure, dealing with people who make fun of you or other kids, or how to get along better with teachers. Include a story about a problem you had and how you solved it.

### NOTES:

**Respect**

Use the power of your feelings to convince people to agree with you, not to beat up those who don't. Respect that there are other sides to issues.

### KIDS WHO RULE

Kids in Florida are taking control of their futures by speaking out against smoking. The state received $200 million from the tobacco industry, and officials are following the recommendations of the Truth Campaign, started by kids under 18, to see how to fight the war against smoking by young people.

www.wholetruth.com

9

# SUGGESTED ACTIVITIES

## SCHOOL SITUATIONS

What are the biggest problems in your school? What are your friends and classmates worried about? What are your teachers and parents concerned about? How do you feel about what's going on, and how would you solve the problems?

### WHAT YOU'LL DO

1. Examine a problem in schools.

2. Learn more about it.

3. Think about how you would solve it.

4. Write about the problem and your solutions.

### GETTING STARTED

⭐ Make a list of the problems people are talking about at school, from bad lunches to school violence and everything in between (use the form on page 12). What is most important to you and the people you know at your school?

⭐ From your lists, pick an issue that you care deeply about. Look for problems that make you feel a strong emotion such as anger, irritation, fear, worry or frustration.

### THINK IT THROUGH

⭐ Brainstorm a list of everything you already know about the topic and how you feel about it. How has the problem affected you?

⭐ Decide what you want to say about the issue. You can talk about how you feel about the problem, explore the causes and effects of the problem or try to come up with a solution. Or you can do all three.

## GO SURFING

Check out the *Education* category in your favorite search engine.

Search by *school problems* or *problems in education.*

- Try to come up with a "should" statement about the topic—a sentence that says something should or should not change or happen.

- Make a list of all the reasons that the problem occurs and everything that happens because of it.

## DIG DEEPER

- You can learn more about the problem from talking to your family, people in your school and people in your community.

- Research in newspapers, magazines, books and the Web. Look for facts about the history of the problem and statistics on how many people are affected by it.

## WRITE IT

- Follow the advice and opinion writing tips on page 9.

- Look at the lists you made in the "Think It Through" activities.

- Circle the most important points that you want to make. Then write them on a separate piece of paper and put #1 next to the most important point, #2 by the next most important point and so on.

- Write a few more sentences about each point. If you researched your topic, include the facts and statistics you found out.

- If you found some people who are on the other side, include their arguments and tell why your side is the correct one (see "Logic" in Notes box to right).

- When you talk about people on the other side, make sure you don't argue with them personally. Respect them and their opinions.

### NOTES:

**Logic**

When you want to persuade somebody, use logic. Logic means being reasonable instead of just being emotional. It's the difference between giving your parents three good reasons why you should be able to stay over at a friend's house and just whining that you really want to.

**11**

## SCHOOL SITUATIONS

Problems I've seen or heard about at my school or other schools:
_____
_____
_____
_____
_____

What I already know about the problem:
_____
_____
_____
_____
_____
_____
_____

What I think causes the problem:
_____
_____
_____
_____
_____
_____

What I think happens because of the problem:
_____
_____
_____
_____
_____

How I feel about the problem:
_____
_____
_____
_____
_____
_____

Names of some people I could interview about the problem:
_____
_____
_____
_____

What I think people should do about the problem:
_____
_____
_____
_____
_____

**USING THE CD**

Copy this page or open and print the form from the CD called **page12.pdf**.

# ADULT AWARENESS

Sometimes kids say things like, "When I grow up, I'm going to remember what it was like to be a kid." What do you wish grownups understood about kids? What would you and your friends like to tell parents and teachers about what life is like for people your age?

## WHAT YOU'LL DO

1. Think about some issues that kids and adults disagree about, such as music, allowances, curfews or e-mail.

2. Pick one to explore.

3. Find out other people's opinions.

4. Offer suggestions for adults about dealing with the issue.

## GETTING STARTED

⭐ Brainstorm a list of issues kids wish adults understood about them. Use the form on page 15 to take notes.

⭐ Think about the times when you've said to an adult, "You just don't understand."

⭐ Think about times parents and teachers seem unfair.

## THINK IT THROUGH

⭐ Look at the issues you've listed and think about which ones are most important to people your age.

⭐ Which ones can you make the best arguments for or against? Which ones do you have the best chance of helping adults understand?

⭐ Pick one of these issues to explore.

⭐ Make another list of what you want to say about the issue, how you feel about it and how you think adults feel about it.

---

### NOTES:

**Perspective**

Perspective depends on whose eyes an event or issue is seen through. A student's perspective might be that the teacher gives too much homework, but the teacher might feel that the amount of homework is necessary.

### KIDS WHO RULE

At age 15, Jason started a Web site to help kids in India with learning disabilities.

Jason tested as gifted, but his grades did not show his intelligence because of his disabilities. He began his site as a place for parents, teachers and other students to share information and experiences.

www.ldkids.f2s.com

---

13

## NOTES:

### Inverted pyramid

Inverted pyramid style is when the most important points are made at the beginning. "Inverted" means upside-down. So, to picture an inverted pyramid, think about a triangle with the pointy part at the bottom and the flat base at the top. The base part of the pyramid represents the most important part of your story. Start with what's most important; then fill in the stuff that doesn't matter as much, and end with the least important part of your story.

## FIND OUT MORE

⭐ Ask your friends how they feel about the issue and how they've handled it with adults.

⭐ Ask your parents or other adults how they feel about the issue now and how they felt when they were your age.

## WRITE IT

⭐ Follow the advice and opinion writing tips on page 9.

⭐ Look at the lists you made in the "Think It Through" section.

⭐ Ask yourself what you want to tell people. If you want to tell adults more about what it's like to be a kid, figure out what is the best way to tell them. How can you use logic to help them understand your point of view?

⭐ Maybe you've learned something about the perspective (see definition in Notes box on page 13) adults have and you can share that with other kids. Or maybe you've figured out a way for kids and adults to get along better.

⭐ Try to think of at least three strong points for your argument.

⭐ Organize your argument by putting the points you want to make in order of most important or most convincing to least important or least convincing (using the inverted pyramid style explained in the Notes box to the left).

⭐ If you want your story to be directed at one person, you can set it up as a letter to that person. You could start by saying, "Dear Mom," and go on to tell her what you want her to know.

## ADULT AWARENESS

Things adults don't understand about kids:
_____
_____
_____

Things adults (parents, teachers or others) and
I disagree about:
_____
_____
_____
_____

What I want to remember about being a kid when I
grow up:
_____
_____
_____
_____

How I feel about the issue and how my friends
feel about it:
_____
_____
_____
_____

How I think adults feel about it:
_____
_____
_____

How adults say they felt about it when they were
my age:
_____
_____
_____
_____

What I wish adults understood:
_____
_____
_____

Names of some people I could interview about the
problem:
_____
_____
_____

Some possible solutions for the problem:
_____
_____
_____

### USING THE CD

Copy this page or
open and print the
form from the CD
called **page15.pdf**.

15

## GROWING CONCERNS

Ask your friends what worries them most about the future and the way the world will be as they grow up. What problems do they want to see solved by the time they're adults, or what issues do they see as the biggest challenges for your generation? Write a story about the results of your poll.

### WHAT YOU'LL DO

1. Find out which problems kids are worried about.

2. Take a poll on a specific problem.

3. Write a story about what you've learned.

### GETTING STARTED

⭐ Brainstorm a list of problems you are worried about (use the form on page 18).

⭐ Ask other kids for their suggestions.

⭐ Pick one problem and write it down.

### ASK AROUND

⭐ Decide how many kids you want to participate in your poll.

⭐ Prepare either one question or several questions about the problem.

⭐ Make interview forms you can use to ask people questions or questionnaire forms you can hand out to people.

### THINK IT THROUGH

⭐ Think about the results of your poll.

⭐ What does it say about how kids feel about problems?

⭐ What should adults know about it?

**GO SURFING**

Check out
www.harriszone.com
This site polls people
13 to 18 years old
for their opinions.

## WRITE IT

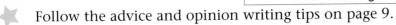

- Follow the advice and opinion writing tips on page 9.

- Write a story in which you interpret (explain) the results of your poll.

- Explain what you found out and why it's important.

- Talk about what it says about kids and their concerns.

- You can include a table or graph with your story showing how many kids gave each possible answer.

### GO SURFING

Check out kidsnews.about.com/library/bl/blpollguide.htm This online guide lists sites where kids can participate in polls.

GROWING CONCERNS

Problems with the world that worry me about the future:

_____
_____
_____
_____
_____
_____
_____

Problems with the world that other kids are worried about:

_____
_____
_____
_____
_____
_____
_____

Group or groups of people I want to survey (for example, kids, adults, teachers, parents, etc.):

_____
_____
_____
_____
_____
_____
_____

Questions to ask (open-ended):

_____
_____
_____
_____
_____
_____
_____

Questions to ask (closed-ended):

_____
_____
_____
_____
_____
_____
_____

**NOTES:**

**Open-Ended vs. Closed-Ended**

See the definition of Open-ended and Close-ended questions in the Notes box on page 51.

**USING THE CD**

Copy this page or open and print the form from the CD called **page18.pdf**.

18

# TAKE A STAND

**W**hat do you feel most strongly about? What issues make you really mad or really happy or proud? Here's your chance to tell the world what matters to you.

## WHAT YOU'LL DO

1. Pick an issue that is important to you.

2. Learn more about it and come up with reasons why it is important.

3. Tell others how you feel and why they should agree with you.

## GETTING STARTED

⭐ Make a list of some ideas and issues that are really important to you.

⭐ Look for things that make you feel a strong emotion— either good or bad. Think about subjects like smoking, school violence, curfews, privacy or grades.

⭐ Think about your opinions on these issues and pick the one that you feel most strongly about.

## THINK IT THROUGH

⭐ Once you've got an issue to explore, think about how you feel and why you feel that way.

⭐ Make a list of everything you believe about that issue (use the form on page 21). If you think something should change, write how it should change. What should happen? How should it take place? Who should be responsible for the change?

⭐ Come up with reasons why you feel the way you do. It's good to have at least three reasons to back up your feelings.

⭐ Include facts to back up your opinions.

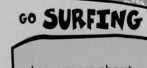

### GO SURFING

Learn more about writing editorials at www.stemnet.nf. ca/snn/ toolbox_opinion. html

19

## LEARN MORE (OPTIONAL)

If you want, you can do some research to find out some facts and statistics (numbers) about your topic.

You can use the library to find books or use the Web (make sure you have your parents' or teacher's permission and see "Online Safety" before doing this).

## WRITE IT

Follow the advice and opinion writing tips on page 9.

Make sure your opinions are strong and clear.

Your story should be organized with your main idea near the top of your story. Your readers should be able to quickly see whatever you think should happen or should not happen.

Include plenty of emotion in your story but also include logic and facts to add power to your writing.

If you have personal experience with the topic, include that, too. That way, you can explain that you are connected with the issue and you can show why you feel the way you do.

TAKE A STAND

hat I already know and believe about the issue
nd how I feel about it:

_____
_____
_____
_____
_____
_____
_____
_____
_____
_____
_____

hat I think should change because of it:

_____
_____
_____
_____
_____
_____
_____
_____
_____
_____

ho should make it change:

_____
_____
_____
_____
_____
_____
_____
_____
_____
_____

acts I've found out that help me make my case:

_____
_____
_____
_____
_____
_____
_____
_____
_____
_____
_____

## USING THE CD

Copy this page or
open and print the
form from the CD
called **page21.pdf**.

21

REVIEWS

YES!

NO!

## CHAPTER MAP

In this chapter you'll pick something to evaluate and tell readers what you do and don't like about it. Activities include:

- Opening the pages on your favorite books

- Telling what's hot and not with trends

- Giving a grade to bands, CDs or songs

- Writing about what's right with the Web

If you see a movie before any of your friends, do they ask you what you thought about it? Do you ever tell them what you thought about the characters, the plot, the acting and the special effects? If so, you've just given a review.

Reviewers tell why they did or didn't like something and what they think other people would think about it. When you review something, you should give details about it and tell what was good and bad about it. Descriptions are based on facts, and evaluations show your opinions.

Here are some examples of topics for reviews:

- The Back Street Boys have a new CD.

- A new Nintendo 64 game comes out.

- You want other kids to know about your favorite book.

### HOW TO WRITE REVIEWS

- Look at the category of the subject you're reviewing (book, movie, TV show or CD, for example.) Think about the best one of those things you've ever read, seen, heard or done. What would a perfect one be like? How does the one you're reviewing measure up?

- Include details to bring your topic to life.

- Be as specific as you can about your feelings. "There wasn't enough action" is more specific than "It was boring."

★ Back up your opinions using facts about the thing you're reviewing. Include the reasons why you felt the way you did. "The plot was interesting because I couldn't figure out what was going to happen next" is better than just saying "It was interesting."

★ Use a rating system, such as stars or smiley faces. Be sure to tell what the highest possible rating is.

★ See the Reviews section at www.kidnews.com for examples written by other kids.

## TIPS FOR REVIEWING SOMETHING WITH A STORY

★ Try to write down the plot (what happens in the story) in just a few sentences.

★ Tell a little bit about the main characters.

★ Focus on why you like or didn't like the plot and what you did or didn't like about it.

★ Look for the conflict (what the main characters are dealing with or trying to get done) in the story.

★ Look for the theme (the message) in the story. What did you learn from it?

★ Don't give away the ending.

In addition to the following activities, also consider:

**Movie Time**: Give your opinions about a movie you've seen. Tell a little about what happens in it. Focus on what you did or didn't like and who you think would enjoy watching it.

**TV Talk**: Pick a show to watch and write about. It can be one you like or one you don't. Tell a little about what the show is about and why you think it's good or not.

**Playing Games**: Write about a video game, board game, online game or any other game you can think of. Tell what is involved in playing the game, what you did or didn't like about it and who you think would enjoy playing it.

GO **SURFING**

You can find reviews of almost anything on the Web, from apples, ext.msstate.edu/ pubs/is1433.htm to yachts www.yachtreview.com

**23**

# SUGGESTED ACTIVITIES

## COVERING BOOKS

What do you like to read and why? Who are your favorite authors, and what are your favorite books? What do you think about the most popular books for people your age?

### WHAT YOU'LL DO

1.  Read a book or story.

2.  Tell a little about it and what happens in it.

3.  Give your opinions.

### GETTING STARTED

★ Pick a book or a story to read.

★ It can be a book of fiction (an imaginary story; something that didn't really happen) or nonfiction (how-to books, biographies, history books).

★ You can use something you've already read or go to a library or bookstore and pick something new.

★ If you need help finding something, talk to your friends, your parents, your teacher, a librarian or a bookstore staff member and ask for suggestions.

★ You could also use a book you've read for school.

### READ IT

★ As you read, try to guess what will happen next. How do you think the book or story will end? Why do you think that?

★ If it's a long book, use the form on page 26 to make notes while you read it. Note the parts you like and how you feel.

★ Think about the main characters. Do you like them? Are they believable? What would you do if you were in the story?

**GO SURFING**

Check out book reviews online at www.amazon.com

Amazon has professional reviews as well as ones from readers.

24

★ Reread any parts that you found confusing or didn't understand.

## NOTE IT

Write down some facts about the book. Look at:

★ Who is the author?

★ How many pages does it have?

★ Is it fiction or nonfiction?

★ What type of book is it?

## WRITE IT

★ Follow the review writing tips on page 22.

★ Write a short introduction, giving some facts about the book and telling why you chose to read that story and a little bit about what you thought about it.

★ Write a summary (a short description of what happens in the story) telling about the main plot details. Don't tell how it ends, though. You don't want to spoil it for your readers.

★ Add more details about what you thought about it and why you did or didn't like it.

★ If it's fiction, tell why you liked the story and whether or not it was believable. Talk about your favorite part or parts of the story and your favorite characters.

★ For a nonfiction book, tell what you learned from it.

★ Make a suggestion to other readers about whether or not they should read it.

**NOTES:**

**Book Club**

Gather a group of four or five friends who've all read the book or story. Have each of them write a paragraph about what they thought about the book, put the paragraphs together and publish a list of all the opinions.

**GO SURFING**

Learn more about writing book reviews at www.indiana.edu/~wts/wts/bookreview.html and www.coe.ilstu.edu/mbgraham/c&i210/bokrev.html

SHELBYVILLE-SHELBY CO. PUBLIC LIBRARY

25

COVERING BOOKS

Title of book:_____
Name of author:_____
Number of pages:_____Fiction or nonfiction:_____

For Fiction
Names of main characters:
_____
_____

How you felt about the characters:
_____
_____

Plot Summary
What happens first:
_____
_____

What happens next:
_____
_____

How the story ends:
_____
_____

Your favorite part of the story:
_____
_____

Your Opinion Of It
Did you like it, why or why not?
_____
_____

Would you recommend it to your friends?
_____
_____

Who would enjoy reading this book?
_____
_____

For Nonfiction
What did you learn from it?
_____
_____

Did you enjoy reading it, why or why not?
_____
_____

Would you recommend it to your friends?
_____
_____

Who would enjoy reading it?
_____
_____

**USING THE CD**

Copy this page or open and print the form from the CD called **page26.pdf**.

# TALKIN' 'BOUT TRENDS

What songs, clothes and words are important to you and your friends? Write about what's hot and what's not at your school or in your city.

## WHAT YOU'LL DO

1. Look at a popular trend.

2. Find out why people think it's cool.

3. Give your opinions about it.

## GETTING STARTED

Think about some of the trends in your school or your neighborhood or town. Look for things like:

⭐ What kids are wearing;

⭐ What types of music they're listening to;

⭐ What they like to do for fun;

⭐ What slang (words that become popular among certain groups at certain times) they're using.

Pick one or more of these trends to examine. Remember that a lot of trends are temporary and what's cool this month may be history by next month.

## FIND OUT MORE

⭐ Find out what other kids feel about these trends.

⭐ Interview people and find out why they like or don't like the trend or trends you're reviewing.

⭐ If you want to, ask your parents how they feel about the trend and why.

⭐ Find out more by reading magazine articles you find while looking on the Web. For instance, you could look up "yo-yos" and see what you can find out about their history and popularity.

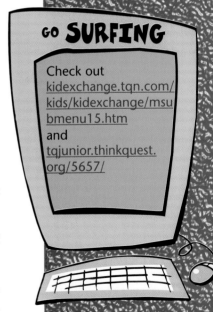

## GO SURFING

Check out
kidexchange.tqn.com/kids/kidexchange/msubmenu15.htm
and
tqjunior.thinkquest.org/5657/

27

## WRITE IT

kidnews.com
submit writing ▼

⭐ Follow the review writing tips on page 22.

⭐ Describe the trend for people who may not know what it is.

⭐ Give some history by talking about how long it's been around in your area.

⭐ If it's a trend that was popular a long time ago and has come back, like tie-dye or hula hoops, include some information about when it was popular before.

⭐ Put in your own opinions about it. If you think it's cool, say so. If you don't like it, though, remember that other people do. Don't be insulting to them; just tell what you don't like about it.

⭐ Include some opinions from other people.

---

## NOTES:

### Go Global

It can be interesting to look into trends in other parts of the country or in other countries. Sometimes trends start in a certain area and then spread to other places. The Web lets you explore what's popular all over the world and communicate with people about what's hot and what's not where they live.

TALKIN' 'BOUT TRENDS

Some trends that are popular right now
(Brainstorm several, then pick one or more to
explore):

_____
_____
_____
_____

Description of the trend:
_____
_____
_____
_____

How you feel about it:
_____
_____
_____
_____

How your friends feel about it? Interview them
and list their opinions:
_____
_____
_____
_____

How your parents feel about it:
_____
_____
_____

Other possible information to include:
_____
_____
_____
_____

How the trends got started:
_____
_____
_____
_____

Where it's popular:
_____
_____
_____

What made it popular:
_____
_____
_____
_____

**USING THE CD**

Copy this page or
open and print the
form from the CD
called **page29.pdf**.

29

## MEASURING MUSIC

What songs or CDs make your toes tap and your fingers snap? Who is your favorite band or singer? What are your least favorite songs? Who do you think sounds like a dog howling in a tornado? Write about music in general. What style do you love or what can't you stand?

### WHAT YOU'LL DO

1. Pick a song, a band or a tape or CD to review.

2. Listen to it and take notes.

3. Write how you feel about it.

### GETTING STARTED

As you listen to a song or CD, try to pretend like you've never heard it before. What do you notice about it?

Listen to the lyrics (words of a song) and try to figure out what they mean.

Make a few notes about what you like or don't like about the song, CD or band.

### LISTEN AND LEARN

Listen to the song or CD a few more times (maybe not that same day) and see how you feel about it. Do you like it better the more you listen to it, or do you start to grow tired of it?

Listen to other songs by that band and compare them with the one you're reviewing. How are they alike? How are they different? Which do you like best?

### GO SURFING

Check out www.epinions.com/musc. You can read other people's opinions and add your own. Make sure it's ok with your parents before you register.

## FIND OUT MORE

★ If you want more information about the band, read the notes listed on the sheet inside the CD case. Sometimes bands will print lyrics or information about the songs.

★ You can also look in magazines, newspapers or on the Web for information about the band, sample songs or other reviews of the CD.

## ASK AROUND

★ Interview your friends and get a few opinions about the band, the song or the CD.

★ You could even ask your parents what they think about it.

## WRITE IT

★ Follow the review writing tips on page 22.

★ Tell why you chose to write about the song, band or CD.

★ If you found some, give a little background or information about the band.

★ Tell what the band is best known for.

★ Write about the specific song or CD you're reviewing. Include information about what kind of music it is, what the lyrics are about and whether it sounds like other songs the band has made.

★ Write your opinions of the music. It can be difficult to write about music because sometimes it seems like all you can say about it is "I like it" or "I don't like it." Try to be specific by telling why you like it or don't. Maybe you like the lyrics, or maybe it's the beat or the singers' voices. How do you feel when you listen to it?

 **NOTES:**

**Rap or Classical?**
You can also talk more about music in general. For instance, you can tell people why you think rap is the best kind of music or why you like to listen to classical music when you study.

### KIDS WHO RULE

An 11-year-old musician named B.J. wanted to learn more about playing the drums, so he checked out some instructional videos. The videos were all for adults, though, and he realized that kids needed something on their level. So B.J. decided to create his own video to teach kids how to play the drums. His dad did a lot of the filming, and they created "Dare to Drum."

www.daretodrum.com

31

MEASURING MUSIC

Name of Band:
_____

Name of CD or tape:
_____
_____

Type of music (country, rock, rap, dance, etc.):
_____

Title of song:
_____

What the lyrics are about:
_____
_____
_____

What the song sounds like:
_____
_____
_____

Your opinion of it:
_____
_____
_____

How it makes you feel:
_____
_____
_____

How other people feel about it:
_____
_____
_____

Information about the band; what they're best
known for:
_____
_____
_____

Names of band members:
_____
_____
_____

Other songs or CDs they've had:
_____
_____
_____

**USING THE CD**

Copy this page or
open and print the
form from the CD
called **page32.pdf**.

32

# WEB SITE SCOOPS

**W**hat Web sites do you like to visit? How did you find out about the site? What do you like about it?

## WHAT YOU'LL DO

1. Pick a Web site.

2. Explore it.

3. Write about it.

## GETTING STARTED

⭐ Once you've chosen this activity, talk with your parents or teacher about the Web and see "Surfing Safely" on page 6.

⭐ Pick a Web site that you really like.

⭐ Make a few notes using the form on page 35. Tell how you found it, what you can do and learn on the site and why you like it.

## SURF AND SEARCH

If you don't already have a Web site you want to write about, use these tips to find one:

⭐ Go to whatever search engine your parents or teachers want you to use. For example, www.yahooligans.com is safe for kids of all ages.

⭐ Play around on the site. Click on some of the category names and find things you're interested in.

⭐ Enter in the name of a hobby or something you would like to know more about and see what results the search engine gives you.

⭐ If you get lost, remember to click on the "Back" button to take you back to where you were before.

### GO SURFING

Check out www.wenet.net/~leroyc/kidsweb/ Three kids, Brian, Mark and Amanda, made this site that lists other sites made by kids.

33

⭐ If you find anything inappropriate for kids to look at, tell your teacher or your parents. If you found it using one of the kid-safe search engines, they may want to e-mail the people who take care of the site and let them know.

## WRITE IT

kidnews.com
submit writing ▼

⭐ Follow the review writing tips on page 22.

⭐ Start with a short description of the site. Tell what its Web address is, what you can learn or do there and what ages it's best for. Here's a form to help.

⭐ Tell readers how you found the site.

⭐ Explain what you like about it. Is it easy to use? Does it have a lot of information? Do you like the way it looks? Be as specific as possible, and include plenty of details.

**GO SURFING**

Once you see enough Web sites, create your own! Check out artforkids.about.com/library/weekly/aa090397.htm for tips.

## WEB SITE SCOOPS

Name of site:
_____

Web address (that's the part with the http://www):
_____

How I found it:
_____
_____
_____
_____
_____
_____

What I like about it:
_____
_____
_____
_____
_____
_____
_____
_____

What I like to do there:
_____
_____
_____
_____
_____
_____
_____
_____

What I can learn from it:
_____
_____
_____
_____
_____
_____
_____

Who would like this site:
_____
_____
_____
_____
_____
_____
_____

### USING THE CD

Copy this page or open and print the form from the CD called **page35.pdf**.

35

## CHAPTER MAP

In this chapter you'll explore your creativity by writing stories and poems. Activities include:

- Opening your imagination to travel through time or invent a world

- Using fiction to deal with real-life situations and problems

- Tapping into your emotions through poetry

## KIDS WHO RULE

Did you know that Stephen King sold his first piece of writing for 25¢ when he was 13 years old? Learn more about kid authors at www.realkids.com/authors.shtml

When writers express what's going on inside their minds instead of focusing on facts, it's called creative writing. Creative writing is about ideas, emotions, thoughts and imagination. Sometimes it explores "what if" and "why" questions, using fiction to help people understand real life. Other times, creative writing is intended only to entertain its audience.

Poems, stories and plays are types of creative writing.

**In a story**, a writer creates a setting with characters and a plot. Short stories usually involve one main character and a few supporting characters with one main plot element. Long stories with many characters and a lot of plot details can take the form of novels or chapter books.

**In a play**, the characters move the plot forward using dialogue and showing action. Plays are usually meant to be performed, so the audience often experiences them through watching and listening, rather than by reading them.

**In a poem**, a poet uses strong images and figurative language, such as similes and metaphors (see sidebar on page 47), to create an emotional response in the reader. Poems usually have short lines and sometimes include rhythm and rhyme. In a poem, a writer uses expressive language, images and poetic rhythm.

## THINKING CREATIVELY

⭐ Let your imagination run free. Especially if you're writing a first draft, you shouldn't try to edit your thoughts or make sure ideas makes sense. Play around with your thoughts and ideas. Have fun.

⭐ Feel your thoughts and think your feelings. If you're not emotionally involved with your story, your readers won't be either.

⭐ Keep an idea journal. Jot down dreams you have, descriptions of people you see, interesting new words you learn and details you observe about places and events.

⭐ Ask yourself a lot of questions. Look at things in new ways. Ask "Why?" and "What if?"

⭐ Experience the world with all your senses. Notice how it feels when you run in new tennis shoes. Pay attention to how the air smells on a cold winter day. These details add life to your stories and poems.

⭐ Read a lot of what you want to write. For instance, if you want to write a poem, read a lot of poetry. You'll find examples that you like and want to use as models for your own poetry. You won't be copying the poems, but you'll be using them as starting points for your own work.

⭐ See the Creative section at www.kidnews.com for examples written by other kids.

## NOTES

⭐ There are lots of places to publish creative writing in magazines and on the Web. Even so, you may want to create stories and poems that are more private, that you don't want anybody else to read.

⭐ One of the most famous poets is Emily Dickinson, who wrote more than 1700 poems. Only 10 were published (without her permission) while she was alive, and no one knew that she had written so many until after she died.

### KIDS WHO RULE

When Kris Atkins was 10, he wrote an essay and rap about improving the environment and was given a seat at the first Kid World Council, sponsored by Nickelodeon. He is now a member of the Youth Advisory Board of an organization called Earth Force.

www.earthforce.org

### GO SURFING

Check out www.inkspot.com/poll/young.html to read advice authors want to give to young writers.

37

# SUGGESTED ACTIVITIES

## IMAGINATION CREATIONS

These stories go as far as your imagination can take you. You can mentally travel backwards or forwards in time and write a story about knights in battle or life on a space station far in the future. Or you could create a fantasy story where your characters may not even be human.

### WHAT YOU'LL DO

1. Pick a setting to write about.

2. Imagine life in that time and place.

3. Create characters to go in the setting and a plot that tells what happens to them.

4. Write your story.

### GETTING STARTED

★ Setting, characters and plot are the most important parts of these stories.

★ Decide on the setting first. Make a list of possibilities using the form on page 40. Do you want to do a story set in the past or in the future? Or do you want to make up your own world?

★ Think about the characters who might be in a place like the one you're describing. Who would live there? What would they be like? When you've made your list, pick a main character.

★ What problems would be caused by the time or place the story is set in? Decide if you want to use real-life problems in an unusual setting or if you want the conflicts to come about because of the setting. Brainstorm a list of possible conflicts and details about them.

★ Sometimes writers use a "fish out of water" technique with stories set in different times. They take a character from the present and send him or her backwards or

---

**NOTES:**

### Short Story Basics

*Characters*: At least one main character and usually several other minor ones.

*Setting*: The time and place in which the story happens.

*Point of view or perspective*: First-person perspective is when the narrator is one of characters and tells the story using "I" and "we". Third-person perspective is when the narrator is not a character and tells the story using "he," "she" and "they".

*Plot*: The action of the story or what happens to the characters.

*Conflict*: Some kind of problem or difficulty the characters are trying to solve, usually the main part of the plot.

*Theme*: The meaning or message; the main point of the story.

**38**

forwards in time to see how life is different. Because this character comes from our time, the audience can usually relate to him or her. These stories are usually written in first-person perspective.

## THINK IT THROUGH

⭐ Make a list of some details about the setting of your story.

⭐ If your story is set in the past, you can do a little research about what life was like then, but don't feel like you have to know everything. For example, if you're writing about the cowboys in the Old West, they can't hop into a pickup truck or turn on the TV, but you don't have to know exactly what kind of cattle they would be herding.

⭐ If your setting is the future, you can make up details about what life would be like. What kind of technology would we have? Where will people live? What will they eat? What will they do for fun?

⭐ Figure out some details about your main character. What type of character is he or she? What is his or her personality? What does he or she look like? Remember that your characters can be people, animals, aliens or any other creature you can think of.

⭐ Decide what the main conflict is in the story. That will be the main point of the plot, the thing the story is about. It can be a conflict between characters or within one character or between a character and the circumstances he or she is in.

⭐ Since a lot of stories that are set in the past or future are adventure stories, you may want to include action and suspense.

GO **SURFING**

Check out
www.netguide.com/
special/living/kids/
story.html
for more information about writing stories.

39

## NOTES:

### Quoting

Quoting means including somebody's exact words in your story. Put quotation marks around everything you quote.

*Punctuation marks:* Only put the subjects actual words in quotation marks. Put punctuation inside the quotation marks. For example: Mary said, "I hope I do well on the test." Or: "I hope I do well on the test," said Mary.

*Ellipses:* If you leave words out in the middle of a quotation use ellipses (...) to show where the words were left out.

*Paraphrasing:* You can use a mixture of paraphrases and quotes when you show somebody else's words. When you paraphrase, you use your own words to show what somebody else said. Make sure you keep the same idea, though, when you change the words.

## WRITE IT

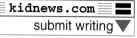
kidnews.com
submit writing ▼

★ You can start with a description of the setting. Include specific details to put your readers in the time and place you're writing about.

★ You can also include a little of the history of the place you're writing about. If there's trouble in the kingdom, you can write a little about how the trouble started, and then lead up to the point at which the story begins.

★ When you introduce your main character, tell how he or she fits into the story. What side is he or she on? What happened to him or her before the story began?

★ Maybe the character won't know any more about the situation than the readers and the hero and readers can learn at the same time. This helps your readers understand your hero and the situation.

★ The minor characters should represent the setting of the story. The main character should be somebody that the audience can relate to, but the minor characters can be more colorful and unusual.

★ Include dialogue to add realism to your story. Put the actual words in quotation marks (see "Quoting" in the Notes box to the left).

★ If you want to write a longer story, you can write chapters and submit each one separately. You can even end each chapter at a suspenseful part of the story so readers will be anxious to get to the next part.

## NOTE

★ Some of the best and most popular books for kids are fantasy stories. The *Harry Potter* series, *The Wizard of Oz*, *The Chronicles of Narnia*, *The Hobbit*, *Alice in Wonderland*, *A Wrinkle in Time* and many of Roald Dahl's books are all fantasies.

IMAGINATION CREATIONS

Explore one or several possibilities for each main feature of your story.

Possible Settings
Explore several; then pick one and brainstorm some details:

_____
_____
_____
_____
_____
_____

Details (what it looks like there, what the land is like, what the buildings are like, what the people are like, what animals are there, what dangers are there):

_____
_____
_____
_____
_____
_____
_____

Characters for the setting:

_____
_____
_____
_____
_____
_____
_____

Details (who the main character is, what he or she looks like, what he or she does, where he or she is from, how old the main character is, who some other characters are, what they are like):

Conflicts for the character:

_____
_____
_____
_____
_____

Details (what goes wrong, how it happens, what problems it causes, how the main character will face it, how it will be solved):

_____
_____
_____
_____
_____

41

## REALITY RULES

Maybe you think lifelike people make the most interesting characters and that actual problems and situations make the most interesting plots. If so, you can choose to write a realistic story.

### WHAT YOU'LL DO

1. Think of a real-life situation or problem you'd like to explore.

2. Create characters for that situation and decide how they react.

3. Figure out how the story ends and how conflicts are solved.

### GETTING STARTED

- In stories of this type, characters and plot are the most important parts.

- To find a plot, you could start by making a list of problems that really happened to you or somebody you know or a situation you heard or read about. Use that only as your starting point, though. You're not reporting on something that really happened, but you can create a new story that's kind of like a situation that really occurred.

- You can also make up a complete new story and use your imagination to figure out what would have happened. Make a list of common problems and questions people face. Which ones do you find interesting? How can you help somebody solve them using fiction?

- Change the details if you use a story that actually happened. You could change the people who were involved in it, the setting, the conflicts and even the ending.

### GO SURFING

One of the most popular authors of reality-based fiction for kids is Judy Blume. Check out her writing tips at www.judyblume.com/writing-jb.html

42

## THINK IT THROUGH

 Once you've decided the main problem in the story, you can start to create your characters. Use the form on page 45 for help in listing details. Who does the plot happen to? Who faces the conflict? Who solves it?

Give your main character a name, a physical description and a personality.

Decide who's going to tell your story. Do you want to use first-person or third-person narration for the perspective of your story? If you use first-person, your narrator is usually a character in the story and is almost always the main character.

You can make yourself the narrator or the main character, but you don't have to. Your main character doesn't have to be anything like you. Men write stories with main characters who are women, older people write stories with teenagers as their main characters, and writers create characters who live in different countries.

If you want, you can write a short biography of your main character, mainly just for your own use to help you get to know your character. Figure out where he or she came from. What else has happened in his or her life? You don't have to include any of these details in your story, but it can help you understand the character better.

Think of some people your main character would know, including friends, family and teachers. Pick some minor characters from this group.

Make a list of the main plot details; then put them in time order. Decide what order you're going to use to tell the story. You don't have to start at the beginning. Some stories start in the middle and then go backwards to explain how the characters got where they are.

## NOTES:

### Reality Books

Other popular reality-based fiction books for kids are the Amber Brown series, the Babysitters Club books, the Junie B. Jones series, and Beverly Cleary's books, as well as older classics, including *Little Women*, *Tom Sawyer*, and *Anne of Green Gables*.

## WRITE IT

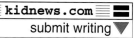

kidnews.com
submit writing ▼

★ You can start with a description of your main character. What does he or she look like? Where is the character from? What type of personality does he or she have? How old is the character?

★ The conflict could already have begun when the story starts, or you could introduce the character at a time when everything was fine, and then bring in the conflict.

★ You could also start with a description of the setting, where and when the story takes place, and then lead into the character and his or her problem.

★ Decide what tone you're going to use for your story. You can make it funny, serious, happy, scary, sad or anything else you want, but stay with whatever tone you choose. Don't try to write a story that is funny but has a sad ending.

★ Include plenty of details and show, rather than tell, readers what they need to know to understand the story. Don't tell your readers that a character is mean; show him or her doing mean things.

★ Use transitions between parts of your story to show movement in time or location. Use words like "next" and "after" to show changes.

★ Include dialogue to add realism to your story. Put the actual words said by characters in quotation marks (see "Quoting" in the sidebar on page 40).

### NOTES:

**Showing, Not Telling**

When you show your readers something, rather than just telling them, you let them see the subject through your eyes. You lead them to understand what you're saying by letting them make up their own minds based on the information you've given them. It's better to show a character doing mean things than it is to just say that he or she isn't nice.

REALITY RULES

Brainstorm several real-life situations (then pick one:

_____
_____
_____
_____
_____
_____

Details (causes of the problem, what happens because of the problem, who might be involved, ways it could be solved):

_____
_____
_____
_____
_____
_____

Characters:

_____
_____
_____
_____

Details (who the main character is, what he or she looks like, how old the main character is, how he or she gets involved with the problem, what he or she does, where he or she is from, who some other characters are, what they are like?):

_____
_____
_____
_____
_____

Setting:

_____
_____
_____
_____

Details (when and where the story happens, what it is like there, what it looks like, who else lives there):

_____
_____
_____
_____

**USING THE CD**

Copy this page or open and print the form from the CD called **page45.pdf**.

45

**What Makes a
Poem  a Poem?**

Poems can have any
of these features.

*Unusual form*: Poems
are divided into lines
and stanzas rather
than written in sen-
tences and para-
graphs.

*Images*: Poets create
word pictures in the
minds of their readers.

*Language*: Poets
choose words care-
fully and use as few as
possible to make their
points.

*Sounds*: Poets look for
words that sound
good together, using
alliteration and asso-
nance and sometimes
rhyming words to add
emotional power to
their poems.

*Rhythm*: Many poems
have a beat. They are
like songs without
music.

*Theme*: The theme is
the meaning or mes-
sage of a poem. Don't
think of it as the
"answer" to the
poem, because there
can be several mean-
ings.

# PLAYING WITH POETRY

Some people are intimidated by poetry, because they think it has to be difficult to read and confusing to understand. They imagine having to create long verses full of "thee" and "thou" and complicated rhymes.

Poetry doesn't have to be fancy, but above all, it should be honest. Poetry is about feelings—emotions and ideas put into language.  If you like playing with words and exploring your emotions, you'll enjoy the unique creative experience of writing poetry.

## WHAT YOU'LL DO

1.  Come up with some ideas of subjects to write about.

2.  Use prewriting techniques to begin exploring a subject.

3.  Add and remove words to create a poetic structure.

4.  Perfect your poem with images, figurative language and rhythm.

## GETTING STARTED

★  Pick a few topics to explore. See the form on page 49 for help.

★  Use a few prewriting techniques to come up with ideas and details about the topic. Brainstorm a list of words that describe your topic, using as much detail as possible.  From you list of words, draw lines from one word to another to start linking images and associations.

★  Explore the topic and see how it makes you feel, what it makes you think about, who it reminds you of, and any other associations you can make.

★  Quickly write a short paragraph about what you want to write about.

**46**

## CREATE IT

⭐ Take your freewritten paragraph and divide it into lines. The lines don't have to be sentences; just break the lines wherever it seems natural. Change lines when something happens or a change occurs. It might be at a comma or a period, or it might be in the middle of a sentence.

⭐ Add some of the images from your list of words.

⭐ Combine some of the words and phrases from your brainstorm with the lines of the paragraph.

## POLISH IT

⭐ Look at every word in the lines and circle the ones that are absolutely necessary, the ones that give details, add meaning and show emotions. Focus on nouns and verbs.

⭐ Draw a line through the words that you haven't circled. Cut out all unnecessary words, especially adjectives and adverbs.

⭐ Read the words that are left, and see where they make sense and say what you want to say. Make any changes that bring the lines to life.

⭐ Add a few instances of figurative language, such as metaphors, similes or personification (see sidebar to the right).

⭐ Look over the individual words and see what you can do with sound. Try changing words to bring in alliteration or assonance (see "Poetic Sounds" on the next page).

⭐ Repeat the steps of cutting unnecessary words and replacing them with important and powerful words.

⭐ You may want to set your poem aside for a while, maybe even a few days, and then come back and see what other changes you can make.

### NOTES:

**Figurative Language**

Figurative language is a way of using words that makes their emotional effect stronger.

Types of figurative language include:

*Similes*: Comparisons that uses the words "like" or "as."

*Metaphor:* A direct comparison that doesn't use "like" or "as."

*Exaggeration* or *hyperbole*: Making something out to be bigger or more important than it really is.

*Personification*: Treating something non-human as if it had human emotions or qualities.

47

## READ IT

⭐ Because poetry is meant to be listened to, as well as read, reading it out loud is very important.

⭐ Listen to the rhythm of the overall poem. Do your words flow the way you want them to? Does it sound like a poem? Are there any places that are hard to read out loud or any places where you feel like the rhythm gets lost?

⭐ Listen to individual words. Remember that your poem doesn't have to rhyme, but the words should have a pleasing sound. Listen for alliteration and assonance.

⭐ Read your poem to another person, or have someone else read it to you, and check for pleasing and powerful sounds.

⭐ Repeat whichever steps of the "Polish It" section that would help make your poem sound better.

## TOPICS FOR POETRY

You can write a poem about anything you want. Famous poems have been written about everything from the pain of war to the pleasure of eating sweet plums. If you need help thinking of a subject, read the list on page 49. It might spark some ideas. Remember, the connection you have about a topic can be positive or negative.

## POETIC SOUNDS

*Alliteration*: Repeating consonant sounds.

*Assonance*: Repeating vowel sounds.

*Rhyme*: Repeating vowel and consonant sounds at the ends of words. In some poems, the last words in the lines rhyme with each other. Don't think that all poetry has to rhyme, though; it doesn't, and trying to force a rhyme can make your poems sound awkward and artificial.

---

**NOTES:**

Listen to poetry read out loud, preferably by the poet. Check out tapes from the library, listen online or look up your favorite poets on a CD-ROM encyclopedia. My favorite poet to hear is Maya Angelou. You can listen to her speak at www.mayaangelou.com/angelou.au

---

**48**

## PLAYING WITH POETRY

You can write a poem about anything you want. If you need help thinking of a subject, read this list. It might spark some ideas. Remember, the connection you have with a topic can be positive or negative.

### Things To Think About

Strong emotions you have felt:
_____
_____

An object that is important to you:
_____

An animal that means a lot to you:
_____

An event that has happened in your life or in history or an event or character that you make up:
_____
_____

A place that is important to you:
_____
_____

A person who has affected your life, either positively or negatively:
_____

A dream or even a nightmare that you have had:
_____
_____

Your future as you imagine it:
_____
_____

A season, holiday or birthday:
_____

A turning point, such as going to a new school, losing a loved one or moving:
_____
_____

Your home and your family:
_____
_____

Something abstract, such as a concept, color, sense or idea:
_____
_____

### USING THE CD

Copy this page or open and print the form from the CD called **page49.pdf**.

49

## CHAPTER MAP

In this chapter you'll learn how to write features and profiles. Activities include:

- Telling about family traditions

- Exploring a hobby– your own or someone else's

- Writing about your favorite places to travel

- Explaining what you admire about your heroes

FEATURES
>click>
>click>

Feature stories are also called "soft news" or "human interest stories" because they are about the people behind the facts. These stories are usually written to entertain and inform, and they don't have to be as recent as hard news.

These stories might include profiles (stories about people and their lives), articles that teach readers how to do something or stories about hobbies or interests.

Here are some examples of feature stories:

⭐ An exchange student comes to your school.

⭐ A friend of yours receives a black belt in karate.

⭐ Your father grew up with 12 children in his family.

## HOW TO WRITE GOOD FEATURES

⭐ Pick a subject that you find interesting; if you like it, your readers will probably enjoy it, too. Your story can be about yourself or someone else.

⭐ Bring in details to involve readers in the story and help them feel connected to the people in it. Include details that show what your subject is really like.

⭐ Show readers why your story has meaning for them by including the emotions and feelings that add human interest.

⭐ See the Features section at www.kidnews.com for examples written by other kids.

## STEPS IN PROFILE WRITING

⭐ Think about all the people you know (including yourself).

⭐ Find someone who is interested in something unusual or has a unique background.

⭐ Ask that person for an interview.

⭐ Prepare questions.

⭐ Conduct the interview.

⭐ Write a story about the person you interviewed.

⭐ Make sure you describe the people in the story— you don't have to tell everything about them, but remember that your readers don't know them like you do.

⭐ Include some quotes from the subject of the profile.

In addition to the following activities, also consider:

**Volunteer Cheers**: Write profiles of people who use their time or talents to make a difference. Find people who volunteer for a club, organization or religious group. Interview them and write about what they do and why they do it.

**Petting Zoo**:  Tell other people about your pet or pets and why they're special to you. Include details about what your pets look like, what tricks they do, how you got your pets, and how they got their names.

**Your Story**:  Write a personal narrative story: a true story about something that happened to you. Pick a memory of an event that is important to you. Pick something that changed your life or made a difference in how you see the world. Include plenty of details to bring the event to life.

**Then and Now**: Interview older relatives, neighbors or family friends about what life was like when they were your age. Write about life before cars, computers, TVs or air conditioning. Compare your life now with life a long time ago.

---

### NOTES:

**Open-Ended vs. Closed-Ended**

In an interview, ask questions that start with "what" or "why." These are open-ended questions.  Avoid questions that can be answered with "yes" or "no." These are close-ended questions.

---

### KIDS WHO RULE

After reading about the shooting of a police dog,11-year-old Stephanie founded an organization called Vest-a-Dog. The program solicits donations and purchases bulletproof vests to protect police dogs. Last year, Vest-a-Dog provided protection to more than 600 canine officers in the United States.

www.vestadog.com

---

51

## SHARING TRADITIONS

How do you celebrate holidays and special occasions? Some traditions are part of your country or your culture, while others are special only to your family. Use this opportunity to learn more about your traditions and share them with other kids around the world.

### WHAT YOU'LL DO

1. Think about a holiday tradition that is important to you.

2. Write about what you do and why it matters to you.

### GETTING STARTED

⭐ Make a list using the form on page 54 of all the details you can think of about the way you celebrate a holiday or special occasion.

⭐ Use *sense* words to add details.

⭐ Write down why the traditions are important to you and how you feel about them.

### LEARNING MORE

⭐ For a family tradition, ask your relatives how it got started and why your family does it. For example, maybe your family opens presents on Christmas morning because you go to church on Christmas Eve.

⭐ For a tradition that is practiced in your country or by your religion or culture, interview your family or a clergyman about how it got started and what it means. For instance, someone from England could find out how Boxing Day got started.

---

### NOTES:

**Sensory Details**

Include sensory details about what you see (decorations), what you hear (special songs) and what you smell and taste (food, incense).

### KIDS WHO RULE

When 12-year-old Lisa was preparing for her bat mitzvah (a ceremony for Jewish girls going through adolescence), she learned about the Jewish tradition of tzedakah or "compassionate charity." Since it's traditional for guests to bring gifts, Lisa asked her friends and family to bring children's books. She received more than 1200 books, and donated them to a shelter that takes in women and children.

www.greatkids.com/stars/profiles/main.html

## WRITE IT

≣ **kidnews.com** ≣ ▬
submit writing ▼

Describe a holiday celebration. It's usually best to organize it in chronological order (arranged in the order of time) using phrases such as "The first thing we do is ..." and "Next, we ..." and to use first-person perspective.

Include plenty of the details you wrote down on your list to talk about things like food and songs and how people are dressed.

⭐ Write about the emotions you feel throughout the celebration. This makes your writing come alive to the people who read it.

⭐ Include any information you've learned about the tradition and what it means to your family or your religion or culture.

## VARIATION

Interview one of your friends about the traditions practiced by his or her family or culture. Compare these traditions with your own or just write about what you learn from your friend.

## GO SURFING

Check out www.rice.edu/ projects/topics/ holidays/festivals.htm for country-by-country descriptions of holidays and festivals written by students.

**53**

SHARING TRADITIONS

The most important holiday to me:
_____

Why I like it:
_____
_____

Feelings I have during this holiday:
_____

What We Do When We Celebrate This Holiday
The first thing we do:
_____

The second thing we do:
_____

The next thing we do:
_____

We also do this:
_____

My favorite part:
_____

Details
This is what we eat:
_____

This is how we dress:
_____

We go here:
_____

We sing these songs:
_____

How the house is decorated:
_____

Why this event is important:
1_____
2_____
3_____

The way we celebrate is special to (choose one
subject) my family, my culture, my religion, my
country:
_____

The tradition began because:
_____

# HOBBIES

Do you know anybody who collects sports cards, rides horses or takes dance classes? Use this opportunity to learn more about somebody else's hobby or write about your own.

## WHAT YOU'LL DO

1. Find somebody with an unusual hobby or interest. (The person can be yourself!)

2. Learn more about the hobby and why the person enjoys it.

3. Share what you've learned with others.

## GETTING STARTED

Pick one of these choices:

★ Think about the people you know who have hobbies. Which are the most unusual? Who is the most involved in his or her hobby?

★ Think about your own hobbies. Which is the most important to you? What would you like other people to know about it?

★ Think about a hobby you'd like to try. Why does it interest you? How can you find out more about it?

## LISTEN & LEARN

If you're writing about somebody else who has a hobby, interview that person and ask questions like:

★ How did you get started?

★ How long have you been involved with this hobby?

★ What do you like about it?

## GO SURFING

Whatever hobby you're exploring, you may find it on the Web. You can also browse the "hobby" category in search engines like yahooligans.com

55

⭐ What equipment do you need?

⭐ Is it an expensive hobby?

⭐ Do you know other people who do this?

⭐ How should somebody else get started?

If you're writing about your own hobby, ask yourself the questions and write out the answers.

## FIND OUT MORE (OPTIONAL)

⭐ For your own or somebody else's hobby, read and learn more from a book or from the Web.

⭐ Enter the name of the hobby in a Web search engine or click on the hobby category and look for it there.

⭐ Try to find an Internet newsgroup for the hobby to find other people involved in it.

## WRITE IT

> ☰ **kidnews.com** ☰ ▬
> submit writing ▼

⭐ Follow the feature writing tips on page 50.

⭐ Describe the hobby. Include plenty of details about what is involved and what makes it fun or interesting.

⭐ If you're writing about someone else's hobby, write about what you learned from talking to that person. Include some quotes from him or her (see "Quoting" in the sidebar on page 40).

⭐ Write about it from the perspective (point of view) of somebody who's new to the activity.

⭐ If you're writing about your own hobby, write about why you got involved in it, what you like about it and how somebody else could get started.

### GO SURFING

Newsgroups are great places to learn more about hobbies. You might have a news-reader on your Web browser, or you can go to www.deja.com to read newsgroup postings.

HOBBIES

Hobbies I enjoy:
_____
_____
_____
_____
_____
_____
_____
_____

Hobbies of people I know:
_____
_____
_____
_____
_____
_____
_____
_____
_____

What is involved with doing the hobby:
_____
_____
_____
_____
_____
_____
_____
_____
_____

Why it's fun:
_____
_____
_____
_____
_____
_____
_____
_____

How other people could get involved:
_____
_____
_____
_____
_____
_____
_____
_____

**USING THE CD**

Copy this page or open and print the form from the CD called **page57.pdf**.

57

# TRAVEL TALES

Where's your favorite place to go, either in your hometown or in the whole world? Write about what it is, what you do there and why you like it.

## WHAT YOU'LL DO

1. Pick a place that you like to visit.

2. Learn more about it.

3. Write about why you like this place and why others should visit it.

## GETTING STARTED

★ Make a list of your favorite places to go using the form on page 60. Include places you like to travel to and attractions you like to visit in your own city or town.

★ Pick your favorite.

★ Make a list of everything you can think of about the place. Write down what you like to do there and what it looks like, sounds like and smells like. If there is a special food you get there, include that.

## FIND OUT MORE (OPTIONAL)

If you'd like more information about the place,

★ If you visited it with your parents, talk to your parents about it and find out why they decided to take you there and what they thought of it.

★ See if it has a Web site by entering the name of the place in a Web search engine.

★ See if your library has any information about the place.

By doing these things, you may be able to put in information that would help other people plan a trip there.

---

## USING THE CD

Keep track of your travels using the form from the CD called **logbook.pdf**.

---

## GO SURFING

See information on writing travel articles, at www.rosengren.net/travel/travelwritingtips.htm
You can find links to sites offering tips on writing and selling.

**58**

## WRITE IT

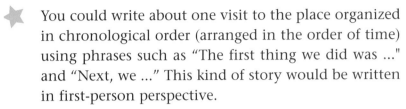

You can choose how you want to write this story.

⭐ You could write about one visit to the place organized in chronological order (arranged in the order of time) using phrases such as "The first thing we did was ..." and "Next, we ..." This kind of story would be written in first-person perspective.

⭐ You could also write it in second-person perspective by telling somebody else why they should go there and what they should do and see.

⭐ Include plenty of details to show readers what your trip was like. Use the details you came up in your "Getting Started" list and write them in sentence form.

### GO SURFING

Keep a daily travel journal while on your trip. For tips, see journals.about.com/library/howto/httravel.htm

59

TRAVEL TALES

Places I like to go:
_____
_____
_____
_____
_____
_____

What I like about them:
_____
_____
_____
_____
_____
_____

What I do there:
_____
_____
_____
_____
_____
_____
_____

Places in my city, town or state:
_____
_____
_____
_____
_____

Vacation spots:
_____
_____
_____
_____
_____
_____

Places I've never been but would like to go:
_____
_____
_____
_____
_____
_____

**USING THE CD**

Copy this page or open and print the form from the CD called **page60.pdf**.

# HEROES

Who do you admire most? From your mom to Martin Luther King, who is your biggest hero and why? Find out more about the person and tell others why he or she matters.

## WHAT YOU'LL DO

1. Pick out a hero—somebody you admire and want to be like.

2. Learn more about that person.

3. Tell others what you've learned and why you admire your hero.

## GETTING STARTED

★ Make a list of the people you admire most (use the form on page 63). They can be people you know or famous people. They can be living or dead. They can even be fictional (make-believe) people or characters.

★ Next to each person's name, write down why that person is a hero to you. What does he or she do? What makes him or her special and admirable?

## FIND OUT MORE

★ Find out some important facts about your hero's life. If the person is someone you know, interview him or her and ask questions about where he or she was born, what life was like growing up, what life is like now, what is important to him or her and who his or her heroes are.

★ If the person is someone famous, use the Web and your library to research the person's biography.

★ On the Web, enter the person's name in a search engine like www.yahoo.com or one of the others.

### GO SURFING

The Web has facts and stories about almost any famous person you can think of. Try entering a name in a search engine or typing in "heroes" to browse through a list.

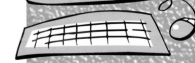

**61**

WRITE IT

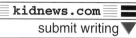
kidnews.com
submit writing ▼

⭐ Follow the feature writing tips on page 50.

⭐ Write a story about the person and why you admire him or her.

⭐ Include important facts and details from the person's life.

⭐ Put in your own thoughts and feelings about your hero. Why do you like him or her? How does he or she inspire you? What have you learned by knowing or reading about him or her?

**NOTES:**

**Provide Perspective**

Since you probably know more about your hero than your readers, remember to tell readers why the person matters to the world.

## HEROES

People I admire:

_____
_____
_____
_____
_____

Why I like them:

_____
_____
_____
_____
_____
_____
_____

### Facts & Details

Famous people:

_____
_____
_____
_____
_____
_____

Family:

_____
_____
_____
_____
_____
_____

Friends:

_____
_____
_____
_____
_____
_____

People from school:

_____
_____
_____
_____
_____
_____

**USING THE CD**

Copy this page or open and print the form from the CD called **page63.pdf**.

## CHAPTER MAP

In this chapter you'll learn how to write stories about sports and athletes. Activities include:

- Reporting on a professional athlete or game

- Profiling an athlete from your school

- Teaching what you know about playing sports

## NOTES:

### Get the Paper

Read the sports section of your local newspaper. Clip the articles you think are interesting and well-written. Start a file for these articles that you can read as inspiration when writing sports articles.

Maybe you love to run, jump, throw, swing, skate, slide, bat and score. Maybe you love to watch other people. Maybe both. Playing or watching sports can take you to the highest highs and the lowest lows. When you write about sports, you capture the excitement the players and spectators feel and share it with other fans.

The best way to learn how to write about sports is to read sports writing. By reading sports writing, you'll pick up the style sports writers use and can try it in your own writing.

Sports writers focus on action, excitement and drama. Often the important part of a game isn't the score. What makes a sports story attention-grabbing is the human interest part— the stories about people and emotions.

Sports stories are easy to find. They're on TV and the radio. They're played at school and in towns and cities around the world. So the trick isn't finding something to write about; it's learning how to write it in the most interesting way possible.

## HOW TO WRITE GOOD SPORTS ARTICLES

Feel the excitement. When you watch a game, make notes about the times that make you jump out of your seat or yell at your TV.

Say it with feeling. Sports writers use strong verbs and try to show emotion in their writing. A team doesn't just win; it clobbers the other team. A player doesn't just hit a home run; he sends the ball into orbit.

★ Include plenty of details. Your readers will want to know more than just what happened; they'll want to be able to feel what the whole experience was like for a spectator.

★ Do some research. Find out facts about the teams, the players and the game to include in your stories. You can find out if a certain player is having a really good season or if he or she is coming back from an injury or anything else that might affect his or her performance.

★ Find out the history of a team. For example: I live in St. Louis, and some of the most exciting baseball games are between our Cardinals and the Chicago Cubs. Fans from both cities really get into these games because the two teams have such a strong rivalry. A story about a Cards and Cubs game should talk about the rivalry and how the fans react.

★ See the Sports section at www.kidnews.com for examples written by other kids.

In addition to the following activities, also consider:

**Sports Challenge**: Pick a sport that you've never played before. Try it, write about it and teach others what you've learned. Find somebody who knows how to play and ask them if they'll teach you a little about it. Write about what the sport was like and whether or not you'd play it again.

**Local Club, League or Team Sports**: Find an amateur team or athlete from your community, interview them and find out how and why they do what they do. Write a profile of the person or team, making sure to include quotes.

**Outdoor Adventures**: Go hiking, biking, rafting, horseback riding, snowboarding or any other outdoor activity you can find, and write about what it was like. Use plenty of details about the place you go to and how you felt while you were doing the activity. Tell your readers how and why they can get involved with the sport you choose.

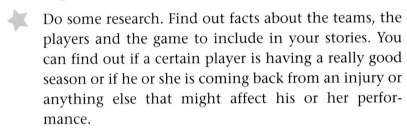

### KIDS WHO RULE

As a freshman in high school, Maren combined two of her biggest passions: soccer and helping other people. She began collecting used soccer balls to donate to organizations for underprivileged kids in her area and has gone on to send soccer equipment to groups as far away as the Ukraine.

www.greatkids.com/ stars/archives/stories/ maren.html

# SUGGESTED ACTIVITIES

## SCOUT OUT THE PROS

Watching professional sports is a thrilling experience. Here's your chance to feel the excitement and share it with readers.

### WHAT YOU'LL DO

1. Learn a little about who you'll be watching.

2. Watch a professional sports game or match, either from the stands or from your couch.

3. Write about what you saw.

### BEFORE THE GAME

- Do a little research about the team or some key players. See what you can find out about records, statistics and who's been making the big plays.

- You can find information about professional sports on the Internet.

Here are a few official sites.

*Baseball:* www.majorleaguebaseball.com
*Basketball:* www.nba.com
*Football:* www.nfl.com
*Olympics:* www.olympic.org
*US Soccer:* www.us-soccer.com

You can find a lot more by using a Web search tool, such as www.yahoo.com, and clicking on Sports.

- Think about the outcome of the game. Who do you think will win? Who do you want to win? Who is expected to win? What is important about this game?

### TAKE A SEAT

- Grab some nachos and enjoy the game, but you won't be an ordinary spectator.

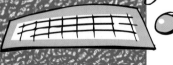

**GO SURFING**

To read professional sports writers, check out *Sports Illustrated for Kids*. Read it online at www.sikids.com For sports writing tips, go to www. stemnet.nf.ca/snn/ toolbox_sports.html

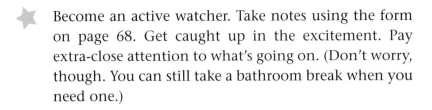

Become an active watcher. Take notes using the form on page 68. Get caught up in the excitement. Pay extra-close attention to what's going on. (Don't worry, though. You can still take a bathroom break when you need one.)

## NOTE IT

As you watch, make notes about what happens. Watch for things like:

*Tense times*—What makes you sit on the edge of your seat and makes your heart beat fast?

*Turnarounds*—When does the momentum of the game shift?

*Big plays*—Who has the moves that bring the crowd to their feet?

*Hard workers*—Who are the players who aren't as flashy but always get the job done?

Listen to the announcers and see what commentary they add. They may fill you in on statistics or player histories that you can use in your writing.

## WRITE IT

kidnews.com
submit writing ▼

Follow the sports writing tips on page 64.

Decide what's important. You can organize your story using the inverted pyramid style (see sidebar on page 14) by putting the most important part—the outcome of the game, for example—at the beginning, then filling in the rest as you go.

Include important facts. You are the expert; you did research before the game, and then you watched it take place. Remember that your readers don't know as much as you do, and it's your job to let them know what happened and why it was important. Oh yeah, don't forget to tell them who won.

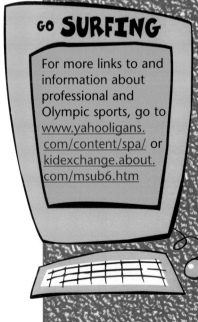

GO **SURFING**

For more links to and information about professional and Olympic sports, go to www.yahooligans. com/content/spa/ or kidexchange.about. com/msub6.htm

67

## USING THE CD

Copy this page or open and print the form from the CD called **page68.pdf**.

SCOUT OUT THE PROS

Teams playing:
_____
_____

Date:
_____

Where the game is taking place:
_____

Highlights of the early part of the game
(inning, quarter, period, half, etc.):
_____
_____
_____
_____
_____
_____
_____
_____

Highlights of the middle part of the game:
_____
_____
_____
_____
_____
_____
_____

Highlights of the last part of the game:
_____
_____
_____
_____
_____
_____
_____
_____
_____

Outcomes (who won, what happens next):
_____
_____
_____
_____
_____

Key players:
_____
_____
_____
_____

# SCHOOL STARS

**W**ho are the heroes of the hallways in your school? Meet the players who make a difference for your school's team and find out how they do it.

## WHAT YOU'LL DO

1. Think of an athlete in your school you would like to interview.

2. Choose someone who works hard and makes a difference on the team.

3. Learn more about the athlete through interviews.

4. Write a profile of the athlete.

## ASK AROUND

⭐ Talk to some other players on the team and get their impressions of the person you're profiling.

⭐ Interview the coach for some quotes about the player.

Here are some sample questions to ask:

What do you notice about _____ during a game?

What is _____ like in practice?

What does _____ like to do when he or she is not playing?

How does _____ make a difference on the team?

What do you think the future holds for _____?

## PRE-GAME PREP

⭐ Ask if you can interview the player before a game. Some athletes like to be alone during that time and may not want to be interviewed. That's ok.

⭐ If you can talk to the player, see how he or she feels going into the game.

---

📌 # NOTES:

### Go Beyond

When deciding whom to profile, think beyond the obvious. Pick a hard worker who doesn't always make the big plays or an up-and-coming athlete.

## KIDS WHO RULE

A hockey fan in San Jose became the youngest person ever to call the action during a professional hockey game. When the San Jose Sharks found out how knowledgeable 12-year-old Justin was, they invited him to the announcer's booth and let him broadcast six minutes of the game. He's now in the NHL Hall of Fame.

www.greatkids.com/
stars/archives/stories/
justin.html

**69**

Here are some questions you might want to ask:

How do you feel right now?

How do you prepare for a game?

Do you have any rituals or superstitions?

## SEE THE ACTION

Watch the player in a game and focus on what he or she does.

Take notes using the form on page 71. Note what you see and feel during the game. Make sure to include a lot of sight details to describe the action. You can also put in details about the sounds of the game (maybe the roar of the crowd or the crack of the bat when it connects with the ball).

## POST-GAME WRAP-UP

If possible, interview the player after the game. If the player or team did not have a good day, keep that in mind when asking for an interview. If the player does not feel like talking to you, respect his or her feelings.

## WRITE IT

Follow the sports writing tips on page 70.

Decide how you want to organize your story and write a rough outline. If you interviewed the athlete's parents, you may want to start by talking about what the athlete was like as a child. If the player had a particularly good game, you may want to start by talking about that. Another choice would be to describe a practice, then lead into the game.

Write a rough draft of your story. Include plenty of sensory details and quotes from the player and those who know him or her.

Revise your draft, making sure you blend your quotations smoothly into your story.

### NOTES:

**Superstitions**

Asking athletes or fans about their superstitions or rituals can be fun; look at things like lucky socks or always eating the same food before a game.

### SCHOOL STARS

Player's name:
_____

Sport(s) he or she plays:
_____
_____

How long he or she has played:
_____

#### During A Game
Key plays the player makes:
_____
_____
_____
_____
_____
_____

What I see:
_____
_____
_____
_____
_____
_____

What I hear:
_____
_____
_____
_____
_____
_____
_____

How the crowd reacts:
_____
_____
_____
_____
_____
_____

What the player does when he or she is on the
sidelines:
_____
_____
_____
_____

### USING THE CD

Copy this page or
open and print the
form from the CD
called **page71.pdf**.

71

## HEREOS & LEGENDS

Basketball became a lot more popular when Michael Jordan flew through the air and slam-dunked the record books. Mark McGwire and Mia Hamm are bringing new fans and players into their sports because of who they are and what they do. For many fans, the stars who play the games are as important as the games themselves. What athletes do you admire the most?

### WHAT YOU'LL DO

1. Pick a star athlete to profile. It doesn't have to be a current player. Legends like Babe Ruth and Mickey Mantle still fascinate fans.

2. Find out more about him or her.

3. Write a story about what you've learned and how you feel.

### READ ALL ABOUT IT

Find out some important facts about the athlete's life. Use the Web and your library to research the person's biography. On the Web, enter the athlete's name in a search engine such as www.yahoo.com.

Pick out important facts such as when the athlete was born, what schools he or she attended, what honors and awards he or she has received, and what are some highlights of his or her career.

### WATCH & LEARN

If the athlete is currently playing, try to watch him or her in action and record some details about what you see and your thoughts and feelings while you watch.

If he or she is no longer playing or if it's not during the sport's season, try to remember a special game or per-

GO **SURFING**

For links to past and present sports stars around the world, see www.starseeker.com/sport.htm

formance you saw and how it made you feel. Your library or video store may have tapes or movies about the athlete that you can watch.

## WRITE IT

⭐ Follow the sports writing tips on page 64.

⭐ Write a story about the star and why you like him or her.

⭐ Include important facts and information about the athlete's life.

⭐ Put in your own thoughts and feelings about the star. Why do you like him or her? How does he or she inspire you? What have you learned by watching him or her? How does watching the athlete make you feel? What has he or she brought to the sport?

## GO SURFING

To learn more, check out the *Subjects* portion of sportslegends.about.com/sports/sportslegends/mbody.htm

73

HEROES & LEGENDS

Athlete's name:
_____
_____

Sport(s) he or she plays or played:
_____
_____
_____

Important facts (date of birth, birthplace,
university attended, team(s) played on, career
highlights, awards received, etc.):
_____
_____
_____
_____
_____
_____
_____
_____
_____
_____
_____

Why I admire the athlete:
_____
_____
_____
_____
_____
_____
_____
_____
_____
_____

How I feel when I watch him or her:
_____
_____
_____
_____
_____
_____
_____

## USING THE CD

Copy this page or
open and print the
form from the CD
called **page74.pdf**.

# You're the Coach

What sports can you do as well as or better than most people you know? Now you're the one who's running, skating, dribbling or passing and telling readers how they can, too.

## WHAT YOU'LL DO

1. Figure out what sport or activity you're an expert in or want to become an expert in.

2. Share your knowledge and offer tips to others.

## BEFORE YOU START

⭐ Think about what you already know. Brainstorm a list of everything you already know about the activity (use the form on page 77).

⭐ Decide what you need to know more about. What questions do you have? What questions do you think your readers will have? Ask yourself how you can get the information you need. Is there a coach or other expert you can ask for help? Can you check books or Web sites for more information?

## PLAY IT AGAIN

⭐ Do whatever it is you're writing about. Take notes about what you do and how you do it. Include plenty of details because even though the activity is easy for you now, you're writing for people who don't know as much as you do.

⭐ Think about when you were first learning. What was different then? What have you learned since?

**GO SURFING**

For sports tips and drills, try www.myteam.com/ysnim/templates/main.jsp?i=/org/MYT/sportsCentral/sportsCentral.txt

75

## NOTES:

**Learn by Teaching**

Sometimes the best way to learn is to teach somebody else. In this activity, you'll not only help other people, you may learn something that helps you, too.

## ASK AROUND

If you want more information, get a few more tips from friends or other sources. Not only will this help you know what to tell readers, but it can also help you learn more.

## WRITE IT

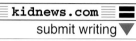

≡ **kidnews.com** ≡ ■
submit writing ▼

⭐ Follow the sports writing tips on page 64.

⭐ Pretend you're helping some younger kids who have never tried the sport or activity you're writing about. Ask yourself what they would need to know. What problems would they have? What would help them get better? What would they be afraid of? What would they feel good about?

⭐ One good way to write the story is as a list of tips.

⭐ Read over your story to see if your facts are correct and your wording is interesting.

## TRY IT OUT

⭐ Have somebody read your tips and try them. Ask a younger brother or sister or even a parent or other adult.

⭐ Fix anything that's confusing or not helpful.

## YOU'RE THE COACH

What I already know about the sport (how it's played, what I do when I play, what can be done to get better, what's easy and hard about it, why I like it):

_____
_____
_____
_____
_____
_____
_____
_____
_____
_____
_____
_____
_____
_____

Advice for new players:

_____
_____
_____
_____
_____
_____
_____
_____
_____
_____
_____
_____

How other people can get involved:

_____
_____
_____
_____
_____
_____
_____
_____

Places I could look or people I could ask for more information about the sport:

_____
_____
_____
_____
_____

### USING THE CD

Copy this page or open and print the form from the CD called **page77.pdf**.

**77**

## CHAPTER MAP

In this chapter you'll learn how to write opinions and editorials. Activities include:

- Explaining what's wrong with school

- Telling adults what they need to know

- Looking into what kids worry about

### USING THE CD

Improve your interviewing skills using the information file on the CD called **Interview.doc**.

News stories are:
*#1*: Reports of events that have happened recently and
*#2*: Events that would be interesting to most people.

If you tell a friend what you did last weekend, you're telling your news. You are talking about events that happened recently. That's item #1. What you did last weekend may not be interesting to people who don't know you, though. That's where #2 comes in.

But maybe what you did *is* interesting to most people. Let's say that your town is near a river and it was threatened by a flood. You spent the weekend helping your neighbors sandbag and protect their property. A flood is the kind of news that is interesting to people everywhere.

Really bad weather problems, like floods, tornadoes, hurricanes and big snowstorms, become national and international news stories. Other news is regional, meaning that it is mainly important to people who live in a certain area. Local news affects your city, town or school.

The following is a list of news stories. Some are local, some are regional, some are national and some are international.

⭐ A famous person dies  (national or international).

⭐ Two countries sign a peace treaty  (international).

⭐ Your school hires a new principal  (local).

Note how some news subjects may be local and as broad as international based on what or who is the subject.

- A building catches on fire
  - ❏ a local warehouse     ❏ Buckingham Palace

- A new mayor is elected
  - ❏ of a small town     ❏ of New York City

- A plane crashes
  - ❏ a two-seater     ❏ an Air Bus     ❏ a commuter

- A new factory is built
  - ❏ to make controversial weapons     ❏ to make toys

## HOW TO WRITE GOOD NEWS STORIES

- Find the news. Look for news that would be of interest to people everywhere.

- Learn more about the story. Research and interview. Learn about the background of a story.

- Make a list of all of the facts and ideas. Number the items on the first list in order of importance.

- Prewrite and plan. Write an outline for your story.

- Write it. Edit it. Publish it.

- See the News section at www.kidnews.com for examples written by other kids.

In addition to the following activities, also consider:

**You Go There:** Find a newsworthy event. (Make sure you have your parents' permission before going to any event.) When you're there, take notes about what happens, what people say and how you feel. Afterwards, interview some people and get their reactions to what happened. Write about what you think will change because of the event.

**Making Your News Newsworthy**: Take an event that happens to you and turn it into something that everybody would care about. Tell what you learned from the experience and how other people could learn, too.

**Hard News vs. Soft News**

These stories are called "hard news" to separate them from "soft news" that focuses on people rather than facts.

### KIDS WHO RULE

When she was 9, Melissa Poe founded an organization called Kids For a Clean Environment (Kids F.A.C.E.) after watching a TV show about pollution. Melissa's letters to the President were printed on billboards across the United States. Now Kids F.A.C.E. has more than 300,000 members worldwide. www.kidsface.org

# SUGGESTED ACTIVITIES

## YOU ARE THERE

**The 5 W's**

The 5 W's are what, who, why, when and where, and the H is how. So the important parts of most stories are what happened, who it happened to, why it occurred, why it's important, when and where it took place and how it happened.

Sometimes news happens where you are. These are events that affect you directly. This is often the case with natural disasters, such as severe weather or earthquakes. It can also be a political or cultural event.

## WHAT YOU'LL DO

1. Experience something newsworthy.

2. Find out how it affected other people.

3. Write about it.

## GETTING STARTED

★ You can't really plan for these kinds of stories. They just happen when you happen to be there. The key is to recognize an event as *news* when it happens.

★ When you witness or experience an event, think about what might make it interesting to readers.

## FIND OUT MORE

★ If an event occurs, the first and most important thing is to make sure you're safe. Sometimes events that are newsworthy are also dangerous. Make sure an adult knows where you are. Don't do anything that could get you hurt or in trouble just so you can get a story.

★ Once you're safe, take notes about the event using the form on page 82. Write down what happened, who it happened to, and why, where, when and how it happened. You can also write about your reactions and feelings.

★ Interview people who were there. If the people were directly involved in the event, they may not want to talk about it. If that is the case, respect their privacy.

## WRITE IT

≡ kidnews.com ≡ ■
submit writing ▼

★ Follow the newswriting steps on page 79.

★ You can write the story in first-person perspective. Since you were there, it's ok to use "I" and "me."

★ Include plenty of details to bring your story to life.

★ Like all news articles, write the story in the past tense.

## VARIATION: YOU GO THERE

If you know a newsworthy story may occur, you can seek it out. For example, if your school board will be voting on whether to make classes last year-round, you can go to the meeting and report about what you learned. In these stories, you go looking for the news with your eyes, ears and notebook open.

## DIG DEEPER

★ Once you've picked a story, check several different publications. By checking many sources, you avoid bias (see Notes box to the right) in your reporting.

★ Ask your friends if they know anything about the story and if they have any opinions about it.

★ Decide what angle (see Notes box to the right) you're going to use to write your story. For example, you could choose to write about how a particular story would affect kids.

## WRITE IT

★ Follow the news writing tips on page 79.

★ Write about why the story would be important to kids and whether kids might feel differently about it than adults do.

★ If you want, give some background information to help readers understand the event. This should come after the main part of the story.

★ Tell readers what they should do to learn more.

**NOTES:**

**Angle**
The angle is the particular way you want to approach the story or the part of the story that you want to focus on.

**NOTES:**

**Bias**
When something is biased, it is unfair, favors one side over the other, or tells only one side of a story. When you tell your mom about a fight between you and your little brother or sister, your story is probably biased. When you write news, you want to be as fair and non-biased as possible.

81

YOU ARE THERE

What the event is:
_____
_____
_____
_____
_____

Where it took place:
_____
_____
_____
_____
_____
_____

When it took place:
_____
_____
_____
_____
_____
_____

What happened:
_____
_____
_____
_____
_____
_____

Who it happened to:
_____
_____
_____
_____

How and why it happened:
_____
_____
_____
_____

How it made me feel:
_____
_____
_____
_____

How other people reacted:
_____
_____
_____

## USING THE CD

Copy this page or open and print the form from the CD called **page82.pdf**.

# LOCAL ANGLE

Some stories happen far away from you but still have an effect on people where you live. Maybe a law changes in your area because of a crime that happened someplace else. Or maybe an event from somewhere else just changes the way people where you live think or feel. In this activity, you'll find out how people near you react to something that happened somewhere else.

## WHAT YOU'LL DO

1. Pick an important event.

2. Learn more about it.

3. Find out how it has made a difference in the lives of people in your area.

4. Write about the effects of the event.

## GETTING STARTED

- Pay attention to the news on TV and the radio.

- Look through the newspaper and see what stories seem to be the most important.

- Look at news on the Web. You can find headlines on the search engines or you can search by "news" and look at stories online.

- Talk to friends, family and teachers about what stories in the news have influenced them the most recently. What events have made impressions, positive or negative, on them?

## FIND IT

- Which stories seem the most interesting? Which ones make you want to ask questions and learn more?

---

**NOTES:**

**Write to the Editor**
Comment on the news in your area by writing to your local newspaper. The paper may have a kids' page or may accept letters to the editor written by kids.

---

83

Think about which stories have had an effect on people where you live.

## DIG DEEPER

Once you've picked a story, read and learn as much as you can about it.

Find out if the event has changed anything in your area. Maybe your school increased its security because of violence at another school.

If the event caused changes, interview people affected by the changes and find out how they feel about it.

If the event has affected your school, talk to some of the people who made the changes. Interview the principal or school board members and find out what went into the decision to change.

If the event did not cause any noticeable changes, talk to people (friends, family, teachers) and find out what they know about it. Has it changed the way they think or feel about anything? Do they think it will cause any changes where they live?

## WRITE IT

≡ **kidnews.com** ≡ ▬
submit writing ▼

Follow the news writing steps on page 79.

For a story like this, you may want to give some background material near the beginning of the story. This sets up the event first, so you can go on to talk about the changes it has caused or how people have reacted to it.

If they are interesting, include quotes from the people you've talked to (see "Quoting" in the sidebar on page 40).

If readers would want to find out more or take any kind of action after reading your story, tell them what they should do next.

GO **SURFING**

Learn about inverted pyramid, chronological and problem-solution formats at www.mtsu.edu/ ~kblake/171/ pyramid.htm

84

LOCAL ANGLE

Stories in the news (on TV, the Web, the radio
or in the newspaper)(pick one):

_____
_____
_____
_____
_____
_____
_____
_____

Changes the story made in the area where it
occurred:

_____
_____
_____
_____
_____
_____
_____
_____

Ways the story might affect people in my area:

_____
_____
_____
_____
_____
_____
_____

People I could talk to about it:

_____
_____
_____
_____
_____
_____

How people in my area feel about it:

_____
_____
_____
_____
_____
_____

## USING THE CD

Copy this page or
open and print the
form from the CD
called **page85.pdf**.

## KIDS VIEW NEWS

Even when you can't report on the news firsthand, you can still make it newsworthy. In this activity, you'll take the news that other people have written and give it a kid's perspective.

### WHAT YOU'LL DO

1. Find an important event.

2. Learn about it from several sources.

3. Think about how it affects people your age.

4. Write about it from the perspective of a kid.

### GETTING STARTED

⭐ Pay attention to the news on TV and the radio. What are some examples of stories on the news or in the newspaper that have made you feel happy, sad, angry, excited or afraid?

⭐ Look through the newspaper and see what stories seem to be the most important.

⭐ If you have your parents' or teachers' permission, look at news on the Web. You can find headlines on the search engines or you can search by "news" and look at stories online (see "Surfing Safely" on page 6 before doing this.)

### FIND IT

⭐ Think about which stories seem to be the most important. Sometimes where you find a story can make a difference in this. Stories that have exciting pictures or videos often receive more attention on television than in print sources.

⭐ Ask yourself which stories seemed most interesting. Which ones made you want to ask questions and learn more?

**NOTES:**

#### Details

Details bring your writing to life. When you include details in your writing, you help readers create a picture in their minds.

Look at the differences in the details in these two sentences:

1. The weather is nice.

2. The sun is shining brightly, a soft breeze is blowing, and the sky is a clear blue with just a few puffy clouds floating by.

Which one makes you want to go outside?

**NOTES:**

#### Perspective

See page 13 for more about how perspective affects your writing.

**86**

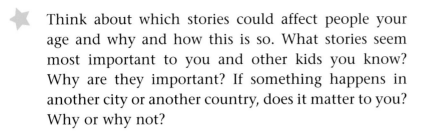

Think about which stories could affect people your age and why and how this is so. What stories seem most important to you and other kids you know? Why are they important? If something happens in another city or another country, does it matter to you? Why or why not?

## DIG DEEPER

Once you've picked a story that would be important and interesting to you and other people your age, read more about it.

Check several different sources in several different publications, so you can make sure you have all the information you need. Also, by checking many sources, you make sure to avoid bias in your reporting. (See Notes on page 81.)

The process of gathering news may sound like one you've used for a social studies or current events class. The difference here is that you're not just telling about what you've learned; you're telling about it from a kid's perspective. Think about why the story is important to kids, what they should know about it and how it could affect them.

You can find this out through the research that you've done or you could interview some young people to get their reactions. Ask your friends if they know anything about the story and if they have any opinions about it.

Decide what angle you're going to use to write your story. The angle is the particular way you want to approach the story or the part of the story that you want to focus on. To write from a kid's perspective, you could choose to take a complicated story and write it in language that kids would understand, or you could choose to write about how a particular story would affect kids and how they feel about it.

GO **SURFING**

In addition to www.kidnews.com, you can read international news stories written by kids at www.cenews.org

87

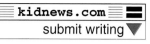

WRITE IT

⭐ Go through the news writing steps on page 79.

⭐ Remember that you're writing this story from the perspective of a young person. You're not just telling what you learned. You're telling why it matters to you and other people your age.

⭐ If you want, you can give some background information to help readers understand what happened before the event took place. This should come after the main part of the story.

⭐ Write about why the story would be important to kids and whether kids might feel differently about it than adults do. Tell why the story is or isn't important to kids.

⭐ If readers would want to find out more or take any kind of action after reading your story, you could tell them what they should do to learn more.

GO **SURFING**

See what adults think kids want to know by reading stories at www.yahooligans. com/content/news/ or www. timeforkids.com

KIDS VIEW NEWS

Stories in the news (from TV, the radio, the
Web, or the newspaper) - pick the one you find
most interesting:
_____
_____
_____
_____
_____
_____

Places to look for more information about the
story:
_____
_____
_____
_____
_____

What I think other kids should know about the
story:
_____
_____
_____
_____
_____
_____
_____

Why the story matters to kids and how they feel
about the story:
_____
_____
_____
_____
_____
_____
_____
_____

Differences between the way kids feel and the
way adults feel:
_____
_____
_____
_____
_____

**USING THE CD**

Copy this page or
open and print the
form from the CD
called **page89.pdf**.

89

# RESOURCES

### Hands-On English
Book uses a visual approach that makes grammar accessible to students who have previously found it baffling.
www.porticobooks.com

### Just Think Foundation
Teaches kids to use technology tools to build media of their own.
www.justthink.org

### Kid Pub
Accepts writing from kids.
www.kidpub.org

### The KidLink Network
Works to help children be involved in global dialog. Programs for teachers and adults, too.
www.kidlink.org

### Market Guide for Young Writers
This book lists opportunities for writers ages 8 to 18 to sell what they write.
Writer's Digest Books
(800) 289-0963

### Ntl. Scholastic Press Assn.
For high school newspaper staffs.
studentpress.org

### Newspapers in Education
Newspaper Assn. of America Provides newspapers for classroom learning and discussion.
www.naa.org

### Nickelodeon
Nick News with Linda Ellerbee Ms. Ellerbee interviews and polls kids about their opinions.
www.teachers.nick.com

### Quality Comes in Writing
Sponsored by Bic, provides contests, activities and other materials for kids, parents and teachers.
www.qualitycomesinwriting.com

### twotoads.com
Provides e-mail filtering for students and young writers.
www.twotoads.com

### USA TODAY Education
Provides newspapers and daily online lesson guides to classrooms.
www.usatoday.com/educate/home.htm

*In Canada:*
### SchoolNet News Network
Open to participation by all Canadian K to 12 students. Designed to stimulate students' interest in the media, current events, social sciences and the media. Includes articles by kids.
www.stemnet.nf.ca

## GO SURFING

200 years after the creation of America's Bill of Rights, Nickelodeon published the Declaration of Kids' Rights at www.nick.com/info/rights

90

# INDEX

# OTHER BOOKS FOR FAMILIES FROM **EFG**

ISBN: 0-9630222-9-6
96 pages (2000); $9.99

## Boredom Blasters

*Hours and miles of games and activities to make time fly*

A fun collection of easy-to-understand games and activities designed for those times when you're on the move but can't move about. With everything from classics, such as *20 Questions* and *I Spy*, to unique ideas, such as *Who's Who in the Zoo?* and *The Claw*, these games bring back memories for parents and build new ones for the whole family.

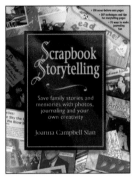

ISBN: 0-9630222-8-8
128 pages (1999); $19.99

## Scrapbook Storytelling

*Save family stories and memories with photos, journaling and your own creativity*

See how to document stories—from a quick sentence to page after scrapbook page. The book is full of ways to recover stories from the past, discover the stories in the present and create stories that light the path to the future.

With easily understood steps for documenting stories, readers then choose to combine narrative with photos, journals, memorabilia and more.

ISBN: 0-9630222-7-X
128 pages (1999); $19.99

## Creating Family Newsletters
*123 ideas for sharing memorable moments with family and friends*

Creating Family Newsletters contains ideas and inspiration that makes a newsletter "doable" by anyone, regardless of age or writing and design ability. Through over 123 color examples, you'll see which type of newsletter is for you—text-only, poems, photo scrapbooks, cards, letters, genealogy, e-mail or Web sites.

## NOTES:

### ISBN

The numbers that follow the letters "ISBN" (listed below the book cover images) are used by booksellers to find and order books. You can find these EFG titles online at:

www.amazon.com
www.booksense.com
www.borders.com
www.bn.com
www.michaels.com
www.powells.com

You can also purchase them through your neighborhood bookstore.

# kidnews.com

## KIDNEWS.COM NEEDS YOU!

Support the ongoing existence of the kidnews.com site by supporting this book. Because each submission is handled with care, the costs of operating the Web site are very high. You support the Web site by supporting this book—its proceeds support the site. Here's how:

**Journalists and media members**: Please review this book and share news of it with your readers, listeners and viewers. We deeply appreciate you showing the book cover along with information on how people can purchase it.

**Publishers**: Mentor the kids and classrooms in your town. Purchase quantities of this book to give as a part of your news outreach to students.

**Booksellers**: Feature this title in your store. It's perfect for the teachers, homeschoolers and parents who care about developing writers and active community members.

**Librarians**: Please request that your library system order copies for each of your branches. You have permission to copy the contents of the CD to your computers.

**Teachers**: Ask your classroom sponsors to purchase copies of this book. Or, request from your school system a purchase of this book for your students.

**Corporate sponsors of classrooms**: Purchase quantities of this book to give to your sponsored classrooms.

**Corporations and foundations**: If the mission of your philanthropic outreach matches the mission of kidnews.com, please contact us about sponsoring and being a part of the Web site and outreach to the media, parents, teachers and students who actively visit the site.

*For more information, contact:*
Elaine Floyd, EFG, Inc.
quicknews@aol.com

## NOTES:

### Mission of kidnews.com

Kidnews.com encourages kids to be active community members through research and reporting their news and opinions. We provide a forum where kids and their ideas are taken seriously and are shared with other kids as well as adults.

## GO SURFING

To see the powerful potential of young writers, see the "Best of kidnews.com" collection at www.kidnews.com/winners.html